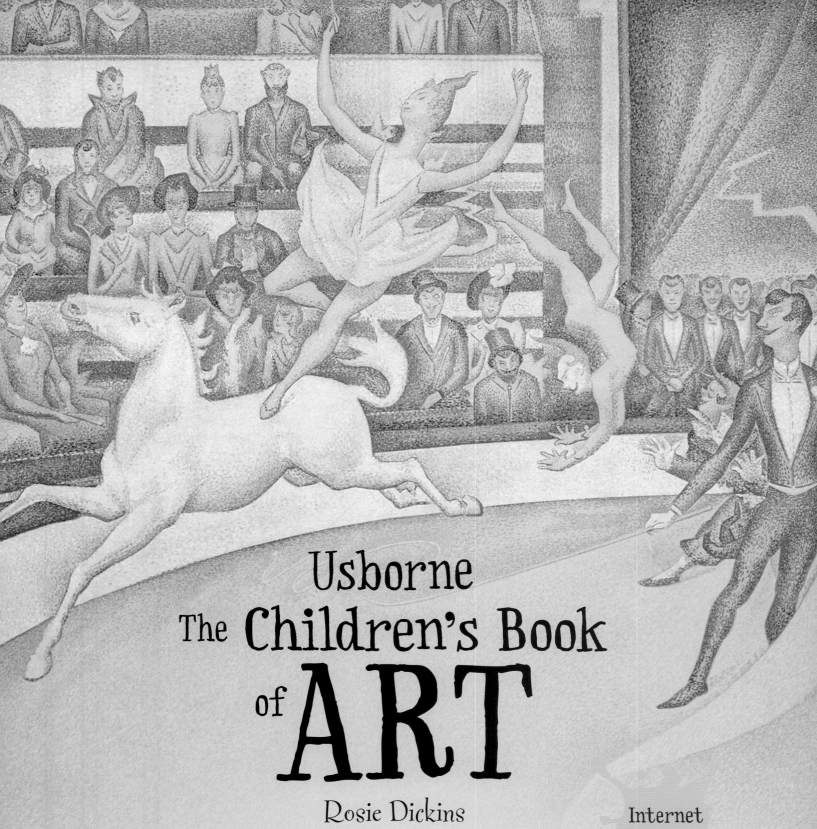

Usborne
The Children's Book
of ART

Rosie Dickins

Internet
Linked

Designed by Nickey Butler
Consultant: Dr. Erika Langmuir, OBE
American Editor: Carrie Armstrong
Cartoons by Uwe Mayer

SCHOLASTIC INC.
New York Toronto London Auckland Sydney
Mexico City New Delhi Hong Kong Buenos Aires

Contents

These pages show part of *The Milkmaid* by Jan Vermeer. You can see the whole painting on page 15.

The picture on the previous page is part of *The Circus* by Georges Seurat. Turn to pages 32-33 to see the whole artwork.

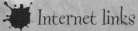 Internet links

Look for Internet link boxes throughout this book. They contain descriptions of websites where you can explore more artworks, play games and create your own art. For links to these websites, go to the **Usborne Quicklinks Website** at **www.usborne-quicklinks.com** and type the keywords "**childrens art**".

Before using the Internet, please read the Internet safety guidelines displayed on the Usborne Quicklinks Website. The recommended websites are regularly reviewed and updated. Usborne Publishing is not responsible for the content of any website other than its own. For more information, please see page 62.

About art

Art is a vast subject, including all kinds of pictures and sculptures. This book introduces 32 works by some of the world's most famous artists. This is only a small selection, but it reveals huge differences in what artists do.

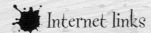 Internet links

For links to websites where you can play art games and find out about art museums, go to www.usborne-quicklinks.com

Why make art?

Artists make art for many reasons. Sometimes, they just want to create something beautiful. But hundreds of years ago – when many people couldn't read – paintings were often designed to illustrate stories, especially Bible stories. And a lot of paintings were made to decorate churches.

Very grand paintings were usually made to order, for wealthy clients who wanted to impress people. More recently, artists have begun to paint to express their own feelings or explore ideas. For example, the painting on the next page was inspired by the artist's love of nature and horses.

Tobias and the Angel illustrates a popular Bible story about an angel who tells a boy how to cure his father's blindness. It was made by a workshop of Italian artists in the 1470s, and measures 33 x 26in.

Detail from *The Birth of Venus* by Botticelli. This is only a tiny section of an enormous painting created for a rich Italian client. Find out more on pages 10-11.

Artistic arguments

People have always argued about art – how
to make it, what it should look like, and why.
For example, some people think paintings should
look true to life. But many artists want to create
more imaginative works – especially now we
have photographs to record how things look.

In the past, artists have fought
court cases, and even duels,
to defend their ideas. But there
are no right or wrong answers.
What kind of art you enjoy is up to you.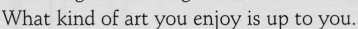

Detail from *The Large Blue Horses* by Franz Marc.
This painting uses bright, unrealistic colors.
You can see the whole picture on pages 40-41.

About this book

The pictures reproduced in
this book were painted over
the last 500 years. They are
arranged roughly in order
of date, so you can see
how ideas about art have
changed over time. If you
would like to see more art,
there is lots on the Internet
– just follow the links
recommended throughout
the book. If you can, visit
an art gallery too, so you
can experience seeing the
"real thing."

Making pictures

There are almost as many ways of making pictures as there are artists. Most of the pictures reproduced in this book are paintings – but there are also drawings, prints, a collage and photographs.

 Internet links

For links to websites where you can find out more about what artists do and try creating your own art, go to www.usborne-quicklinks.com

Different kinds of pictures

There are a lot of different kinds of pictures and picture-making materials. Here are some common ones you will come across in this book.

Oil paintings are made using glossy, slow-drying **oil paints**. These paints are based on "drying oils" such as linseed or walnut oil, which harden slowly when exposed to the air.

Pastel drawings are made using soft crayons known as **pastels**.

Some paintings are made using fast-drying, egg-based paints known as **tempera**.

Paintings can also be made using water-based paints – either transparent paints known as **watercolors** or opaque (not transparent) paints known as **gouache**.

Prints are made using carved blocks or stencils (templates with holes cut in them). Blocks are coated with ink and pressed onto paper. Stencils are laid over paper and spread with ink, so the ink prints through the holes.

Frescos are wall paintings, made by painting watercolors onto wet plaster.

Collages are made by gluing down bits of paper or other materials.

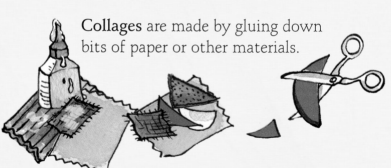

The oil revolution

When oil paints were invented, they revolutionized art. Unlike earlier tempera paints, they take a long time to dry, so artists can work slowly. And since most oil paints are translucent (slightly transparent), artists can build up colors gradually, in layers. This is great for delicate shading and fine details, allowing artists to create incredibly lifelike pictures.

Here you can see tubes of oil paint and a mixing palette.

Mixing oils

Oil paints were first developed in northern Europe in the 14th and 15th centuries, by artists such as Jan van Eyck, who worked in the town of Bruges in Belgium. You can see one of his pictures on the left.

Until about 150 years ago, artists had to make their paints by hand, grinding up colors and mixing them with drying oils. But today, you can buy ready-mixed paint in tubes.

Man in a Turban by Jan van Eyck. This oil painting dates from 1433 and measures 13 x 10in. It is probably a portrait of the artist, or self portrait. You can see how well van Eyck captured the effect of light falling across the face.

7

Renaissance stars

Leonardo painted the *Mona Lisa* between about 1505 and 1514. He used oil paints on a wooden panel measuring 30 x 21in.

In the 15th and 16th centuries, there were lots of new discoveries in art and science. This period is known as the Renaissance. Many star Renaissance artists worked in Italy, including Leonardo da Vinci and Michelangelo Buonarroti. Today, they are seen as two of the greatest artists ever to have come out of Europe.

Smile, please

This woman has one of the most famous faces in the world. But no one knows who she was. Leonardo spent years on her portrait – now known as the *Mona Lisa*. He painted her with delicate, almost invisible brushstrokes, deliberately blurring the corners of her eyes and mouth to give her a mysterious smile.

About Leonardo

Leonardo was born in the small Italian town of Vinci, which is how he got his name – "da Vinci" means "from Vinci." He was interested in science and engineering as well as art, and filled notebooks with hundreds of designs. He even designed a flying machine (though it could never have flown).

8

About Michelangelo

Michelangelo came from the Italian city of Florence. He is famous for sculptures as well as paintings, and he was very good at creating strong, muscular bodies. In fact, his art shows he knew a lot about anatomy, which he probably discovered by dissecting dead bodies.

Divine inspiration

Michelangelo's admirers called him the "Divine Michelangelo." One of his greatest achievements was decorating the ceiling of the Sistine Chapel in the Vatican palace, in Rome. He covered it with more than 3,000 figures illustrating scenes from the Bible. The work took four years – most of which he spent flat on his back on a platform just below the ceiling. It was so uncomfortable, he wrote poems about it.

This section of the Sistine Chapel ceiling shows God bringing Adam, the first man, to life. It is just a tiny fraction of the whole fresco, which Michelangelo worked on from 1508-12.

Internet links

For links to websites where you can find out more about Leonardo and Michelangelo, go to www.usborne-quicklinks.com

9

The Birth of Venus

This picture shows Venus, the Roman goddess of love. The story goes that she was born from a shell, like a pearl. She is standing on the shell while two wind gods blow her to shore, where an attendant waits with a cloak. Notice the shower of roses, which legend says were created at her birth.

The Birth of Venus was painted in 1485 by Sandro Botticelli. He used tempera on canvas. The picture measures 68 x 110in.

Spot the mistake

Venus is amazingly beautiful. But, if you look closely, do you notice something slightly strange about her neck and shoulders?

Venus' body is distorted. Her neck is oddly long and her shoulders slope far too steeply. In fact, her left shoulder has nearly disappeared. You might think the artist made a mistake drawing her like this. But he probably did it on purpose, to create a more graceful, flowing shape.

Golden touch

The sparkling highlights on the roses and trees are made out of real gold. This shows how precious the picture was, and stresses the importance of Venus as a goddess.

About Botticelli

Sandro Botticelli was born in Italy in about 1445. His real name was Alessandro Filipepi. "Botticelli" was his nickname. It means "little barrel" in Italian. Botticelli painted Venus for the palace of a rich young Italian, who was interested in Roman myths. The story of Venus had just been retold by an Italian poet, and the picture is a silent version of the poem.

Internet links
For a link to a website where you can view more pictures by Botticelli, go to www.usborne-quicklinks.com

Hunters in the Snow

Pieter Bruegel painted *Hunters in the Snow* in 1565. He used oil paints on a wooden panel measuring 46 x 64in.

 Internet links

For links to websites where you can see more pictures by Bruegel and find out about colors, go to **www.usborne-quicklinks.com**

This picture shows a group of hunters trudging home through thick winter snow. In the background, more people are going about their daily lives – cooking over a fire or skating on a frozen lake. It looks very lifelike, but it's an imaginary scene. For instance, the houses are Flemish, but the Flemish landscape is really very flat. The artist, Pieter Bruegel, added mountains to make it look more interesting.

Warm and cool

Bruegel deliberately filled his picture with wintry blues and greens. These are known as "cool" colors because they are the colors of water and ice, and make things feel chilly. Reds and oranges are known as "warm" colors because they are the colors of fire and sunshine, and make things look warm. The orangey flames of the fire seem to blaze with heat. Bruegel also used warm colors on some of the houses and dogs, making them stand out from the frozen landscape.

Try comparing these cartoons and see how the different colors make you feel.

About Bruegel

Pieter Bruegel lived in part of Flanders (now in Belgium) in the 16th century. He is famous for painting country scenes. Often he is known as Bruegel the Elder, to distinguish him from his children and grandchildren, who became artists too.

Everyday scenes

In 17th-century Holland, there was a craze for scenes of ordinary life, filled with realistic details – such as these two pictures showing an artist and a milkmaid going about their daily work.

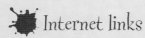 Internet links

For links to websites where you can take a tour of Rembrandt's house or solve a Vermeer jigsaw puzzle, go to www.usborne-quicklinks.com

Rembrandt painted *The Artist in his Studio* in about 1627-28. He used oil paints on a wooden panel measuring just 10 x 13in.

Artist at work

This painting of Rembrandt in his studio has many lifelike touches, from the artist's tools to the cracks in the walls. His fancy-looking robe is in fact an ordinary housecoat, which he wore to keep warm. The focus of the scene is the panel on his easel. Its edge glows in the light – but teasingly, you can't see the picture on it.

About Rembrandt

Harmensz van Rijn Rembrandt was born in Holland in 1606. He became one of the leading artists of his time. He made most of his money by painting portraits, but fell out with his clients and died, bankrupt, in 1669.

Rembrandt painted more than 60 self portraits during his life.

Jan Vermeer painted *The Milkmaid* in about 1658-60. He used oil paints on a canvas measuring 18 x 16in.

Notice the traditional Dutch tiles along the skirting board. The box beside them would be filled with hot coals, as a kind of foot warmer.

About Vermeer

Jan Vermeer was born in Holland in 1632. He was an art dealer as well as a painter, but never sold many of his own pictures – though they are priceless now. When he died in 1675, most of them were still in his house.

The Milkmaid

Vermeer is famous for the way he captured light. It is the light falling from the window and catching the trickling milk that brings this scene to life. It is painted so accurately, it almost looks like a photograph. Experts think Vermeer used a kind of early camera to help him draw.

Fruit and Flowers

Some painters specialize in arrangements of fruit, flowers and other objects, known as still lifes. In 18th-century Holland, there was a fashion for still lifes showing collections of luxury items, as in the picture on the right. It contains a pineapple – then a rare, expensive fruit – and tulips, which were so highly prized that some collectors would give their life savings for a single bulb.

Dutch painter Jan van Os painted *Fruit and Flowers in a Terracotta Vase* between 1777 and 1778. He used oil paints on a mahogany panel measuring 35 x 28in.

About van Os

Jan van Os was born in Holland in 1744. Still lifes had become very popular there and van Os painted them by the dozen, becoming known for the unusual arrangements he liked to create. His two sons, Giorgius and Pieter, became artists too. Van Os died in 1808.

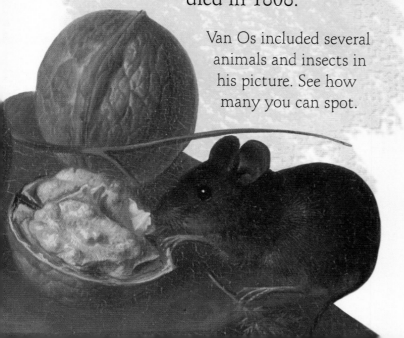

Van Os included several animals and insects in his picture. See how many you can spot.

A dazzling display

The display on the right looks dazzlingly lifelike. But, in fact, it was put together in the artist's imagination. Look at the pineapple in the top-right corner. It adds a dramatic flourish to the arrangement – but if it had really been there, it would have toppled over.

Also, no one could have seen all these flowers and fruits together. Tulips bloom in the spring and roses in the summer, while most of the fruits only appear in the fall. The artist, Jan van Os, built up the picture over a whole year, adding each plant as it came into season.

Internet links

For links to websites where you can find out more about still life paintings, go to **www.usborne-quicklinks.com**

Perfect portraits

Francisco de Goya earned fame and fortune painting beautiful portraits of Spain's rich, fashionable elite. But he also excelled at another, very different kind of art – grotesque prints mocking the faults he saw in the world around him. Nothing escaped his critical eye, not even himself.

Goya must have painted *Doña Isabel de Porcel* in the early 1800s. The finished portrait was exhibited in Madrid in 1805.

Goya used oil paints on a canvas measuring 32 x 22in. It was an old canvas that he was reusing. X-rays show a painting of a man in uniform underneath.

Fashion and flattery

The portrait on the left is of a wealthy Spanish lady named Doña Isabel de Porcel. She is dressed up in a kind of folk costume then the height of fashion in Madrid. Goya painted her with soft, flattering brushstrokes, using the black lace of her shawl to show off her fresh pink coloring.

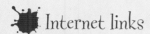 Internet links

For links to websites with information and games about portraits, go to **www.usborne-quicklinks.com**

About Goya

Francisco de Goya was born in Spain in 1746. After studying art, he became one of the top portrait painters of his day. He moved to Madrid and was appointed official court painter to three generations of Spanish kings. But later, Goya fell out of favor. He even got into trouble with the Inquisition (a religious court), because he had once painted a nude woman. He died in France in 1828.

Cheeky monkey

This print of a monkey painting a donkey shows Goya poking fun at his own profession. The donkey poses proudly, hogging the light, while the monkey-artist crouches humbly in the dark. The monkey's picture flatters the donkey by hiding its huge ears. But, in reality, the donkey looks awkward and silly. Goya called the print *Neither More Nor Less*. The title is probably a sarcastic reference to the accuracy of most fashionable portraits.

Goya created *Neither More Nor Less* in the 1700s. It measures just 8 x 6in.

Wanderer Above the Sea of Fog

This atmospheric mountain scene was painted in Germany nearly 200 years ago. It shows rocky crags and peaks rising dramatically out of the mist. But the focus of the picture is a solitary figure standing with his back to us.

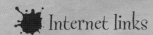

Internet links

For links to websites where you can see more paintings by Friedrich and make a landscape picture of your own, go to www.usborne-quicklinks.com

About Friedrich

Caspar David Friedrich was born in Germany in 1774. His mother died when he was only seven, and his father brought him up to be very religious.

After studying art, Friedrich moved to Dresden, in northern Germany. Many of his landscapes were inspired by the woods, hills and ruined abbey buildings near Dresden. His paintings were often meant to inspire religious feelings. He died in 1840.

Awesome scene

The wanderer's face is hidden, making viewers wonder about his reaction to the stunning scenery in front of him. He seems to be lost in thought, perhaps struck with awe. With his frock coat and stick, some art experts have suggested he is a portrait of the artist, Caspar David Friedrich, himself. His dark, upright figure forms a bold contrast with the misty peaks and distant horizon.

Romantic views

Friedrich is often described as a "Romantic" artist – not because he painted lovey-dovey scenes, but because of the way his pictures seem to be about people's feelings towards nature. Personal feelings – especially a love of nature – inspired a group of 19th-century artists and writers known as Romantics.

Friedrich painted *Wanderer Above the Sea of Fog* in 1818, using oil paints on canvas. It measures 37 x 30in.

21

Ophelia

This painting was inspired by Shakespeare's play, *Hamlet*. In the play, Hamlet kills Ophelia's father. Insane with grief, she goes to pick flowers, falls into a stream and drowns. Her tragic death was a popular subject for artists in the 19th century.

Ophelia was painted in 1851-52 by John Millais. He used oil paints on a canvas measuring 30 x 44in.

About Millais

John Everett Millais was born in England in 1829. He began studying art at London's Royal Academy at the age of 11. Later, he helped found a movement known as the Pre-Raphaelite Brotherhood. The Brotherhood wanted to make art that was both spiritual and true to nature. So they always worked from life, and often chose subjects from the Bible or classic stories.

True to life

Milliais did his best to make his pictures appear true-to-life. For this scene, he spent months painting by the Hogsmill river in southern England – despite being tormented by mosquitoes and unfriendly landowners.

Achoo!

Millais went back to his London studio to paint Ophelia. But to make her look authentic, he got his model, Lizzie Siddal, to wear an old embroidered dress and lie in a bathtub full of water for hours on end.

The bathwater got so chilly that Lizzie caught a dreadful cold.

Blooming marvellous

Although the scene seems very lifelike, the flowers in it bloom at different times of year. So Millais never saw them together like this. He chose them because they are mentioned in the play and have symbolic meanings. For example, roses stand for beauty and love, and violets for faithfulness. The tree in the background is a weeping willow – a traditional symbol of unhappy love.

Moody landscapes

Some painters specialize in moody, evocative views of land, sea and sky. Two 19th-century artists famous for their mood-filled landscapes were Whistler and Turner.

Nocturne in Blue and Silver

Whistler often gave his paintings vague, suggestive titles such as this *Nocturne,* or "night scene." It shows a misty world with only a shadowy boat and a few lights to hint at its subject – Battersea, in London.

Whistler painted *Nocturne in Blue and Silver: Battersea Reach* in the 1870s. He used oil paints on a canvas of 15 x 25in.

Whistler's daringly sketchy style didn't please everyone, though. One critic even accused him of "flinging a pot of paint in the public's face." Furious, Whistler sued for libel – and won, although the cost of the case left him almost bankrupt.

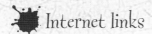 Internet links

For links to websites with more moody landscapes and games, go to www.usborne-quicklinks.com

About Turner and Whistler

James Whistler was born in the U.S. in 1834. After failing military college, he went to Paris to study art, developing a style of painting focused on color. Later, he moved to London, where he died in 1903.

J.M.W. Turner was born in England in 1775. A barber's son, he exhibited his first works in his father's shop. He hated publicity and, as his fame grew, hid behind the false name "Admiral Booth." He died in 1851.

The "Fighting Temeraire"

This picture shows a tug towing an old warship away for scrap. Turner saw this happen – but when he painted it, he changed parts to make it more dramatic. The *Temeraire* had lost its masts, but Turner drew them in, exaggerating the contrast between the tall, graceful warship and the squat, steam-belching tug. He also added a glowing sunset, to give a feeling of ending and loss.

Turner loved watching weather. He once tied himself to a ship's mast so he could sketch a storm.

The "Fighting Temeraire" Tugged to Her Last Berth to be Broken Up, 1838 was painted by Turner in 1839. He used oil paints on a canvas measuring 35 x 48in. Critics heaped praise on the finished picture. Turner called it his "darling" and refused to sell it.

Ballet dancers

Edgar Degas was fascinated by ballet dancers. He made over 1,500 paintings and drawings of them, as well as dozens of sculptures. He showed them in many poses – not just dancing, but going to classes, chatting, stretching and tying their shoes.

Little Dancer

Degas made *Little Dancer Aged Fourteen* in 1880-81. She stands just 39in high. Degas made a wax figure, which was then cast in bronze, and gave her a real cloth skirt and hair ribbon.

The model for this sculpture was a young dance student named Marie van Goethen. Compared to the elegant ballerina opposite, she looks stiff and awkward. You can even see wrinkles in her stockings. Most artists preferred to draw or sculpt models in graceful-looking poses. But Degas wanted to show how people really move, catching them in just the awkward, unbalanced poses other artists avoided.

Internet links
For links to websites where you can find out more about Degas and his dancers, go to www.usborne-quicklinks.com

About Edgar Degas

Edgar Degas was born in France in 1834 and studied law before taking up art. He specialized in painting dancers and racehorses, and women washing themselves. As he grew older, he suffered eye problems and began to make more sculptures instead.

Dancer on the Stage

This pastel drawing shows a leading ballerina in the middle of a dance. She is lit from below by footlights, which cast strange shadows on her face. Degas drew her oddly off-center, from an angle that lets you see past the scenery and into the wings. All this helps capture the atmosphere of a real performance, watched from a box beside the stage.

You can see Degas' pastel marks clearly in this enlarged detail.

Degas drew *Dancer on the Stage* in 1878, using pastels on a piece of paper sized 24 x 17in. He called his method "drawing with color" – meaning he built up shapes with dabs of different colored pastels, rather than starting with outlines.

The Water Lily Pond

Monet painted *The Water Lily Pond* in 1899, using oil paints on canvas. It measures 35 x 37in.

Claude Monet loved to paint the pond in his garden. This view shows it in early summer, with sunlight catching the lilies and leaves, and glinting off the Japanese-style bridge.

Making an impression

Monet liked to paint fast and outdoors, so he could capture the changing effects of light and weather. Compared to many other artists, his pictures are like quick "impressions" – which made art critics call this style Impressionism.

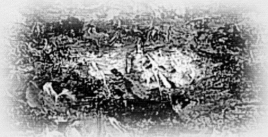

You can see Monet's rapid, sketchy brush strokes in this detail.

Lots of lily pictures

Monet painted his lily pond over and over again. In fact, he is famous for making series of paintings showing the same scene in different conditions.

About Monet

Claude Monet was born in France in 1840. As a young artist, he pioneered the style known as Impressionism. At first people mocked his sketchy, atmospheric paintings. But, by the time Monet died in 1926, he was one of the world's most successful artists.

Monet once had a tree's leaves removed, so he could finish painting a winter scene.

He enjoyed watching how things change between dawn and dusk, or summer and winter, seeing color and light in even the bleakest winter landscape.

Monet designed his garden himself. This photograph shows it as it looks today.

Sunflowers

In 1888, Dutch artist Vincent van Gogh moved to Arles, in the south of France, attracted by the sunny southern landscape – especially its fields full of sunflowers.

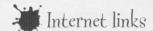 Internet links

For links to websites with more pictures by van Gogh and Gauguin, go to www.usborne-quicklinks.com

Van Gogh painted *Sunflowers* in 1888, using oil paints on canvas. He chose bright, modern paint colors, often applying paints straight from the tube. The picture measures 36 x 29in.

A welcoming picture

Van Gogh loved the local sunflowers and painted them again and again, working rapidly in thick, bumpy layers of paint. He used the paintings to decorate his house and welcome his friend, the artist Paul Gauguin, who came to stay with him in Arles.

The picture on the left shows a dozen flowers crammed into a small clay jar. They are meant to dazzle viewers with their brilliant color. Van Gogh also believed colors were symbolic and, to him, yellow represented happiness and friendship.

Van Gogh Painting

This picture by Gauguin shows van Gogh working on one of his sunflower paintings. Gauguin can't really have seen this, as the sunflowers weren't in bloom while he was in Arles. But he liked to paint from memory and imagination – unlike van Gogh, who preferred to paint from life.

Gauguin created *Van Gogh Painting Sunflowers* in November 1888. He used oil paints on a canvas measuring 29 x 37in.

At the time of this portrait, the two friends had begun to quarrel. A month later, they had a violent argument and van Gogh threatened Gauguin with a knife. Gauguin fled Arles, never to return. Terribly upset, van Gogh turned the knife on himself and cut off part of his own ear.

About van Gogh and Gauguin

Vincent van Gogh was born in Holland in 1853. His paintings are worth millions today, but he only managed to sell one in his life. He suffered from mental illness and killed himself in 1890.

Paul Gauguin was born in France in 1848. He worked as a sailor and stockbroker before becoming an artist. People admired his style, but he struggled to make a living from art. He died in Tahiti in 1903.

Gauguin spent several years painting in Tahiti.

The Circus

This colorful circus scene was painted by Georges Seurat in 1890-91. Seurat copied the horse, rider and clown from actual circus posters. But he painted them in his own particular way, following new scientific ideas about how we see light and color.

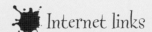 Internet links

For links to websites where you can explore another painting by Seurat or play a game about colors, go to www.usborne-quicklinks.com

Going dotty

If you look closely at the painting, you can see it is made up of thousands of colored dots. But, from a distance, the dots seem to merge and form new blended colors. Seurat believed these colors would appear brighter and more vivid, because the mixing is done not with paint but with light in the viewer's eye.

One of his fellow artists described the technique as "painting with jewels." It became known as Pointillism.

About Seurat

Georges Seurat was born in 1859 in France. He became known for painting with dots. This method was very slow and his pictures were often huge, so it could take him years to complete one. *The Circus* was his last big painting, but he never completely finished it. It was exhibited in Paris in 1891. Seurat died during the exhibition, aged only 31.

You can see the dots more clearly in this detail. Seurat dabbed on each dot separately, using just the tip of his brush.

Notice how Seurat avoided using black. The dark areas are actually made up of blue dots.

Seurat painted *The Circus* using oil paints on canvas. But he didn't just paint the canvas – he painted the picture frame too. The whole artwork measures 73 x 59in, making it as tall as a man.

The man in the front row wearing a top hat was one of Seurat's friends, Charles Angrand.

Color wheel

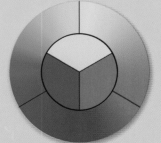

The wheel is made up of the "primary" colors red, yellow and blue, and the colors you get by mixing them. Each color lies opposite its complementary, giving three main pairs: red/green, orange/blue and yellow/purple.

Bright ideas

Some pairs of colors are known as complementary colors. Seen side by side, they contrast very strongly and make each other look brighter. You can determine the pairs using a color wheel (see right). Seurat deliberately used them in his art, for example by combining blue and orange dots.

This painting is full of drama, with its crouching tiger and stormy skies. But it is like a scene from a dream. Everything is oddly flat and the tiger balances awkwardly on the leaves.

Imaginary travels

The artist, Henri Rousseau, loved painting tropical places, but he never really went to any. Instead, he made sketches in local parks and zoos, and used his imagination. Some of the plants in this scene were actually based on ornamental houseplants.

Does it matter if Rousseau made things up? Some people think the strange, dreamlike quality of his pictures comes from the way he had to imagine everything. And perhaps it is just as well this scene isn't real. According to Rousseau, the tiger in this picture was about to pounce on some unlucky explorers.

Tiger in a Tropical Storm – Surprise! was made using oil paints on canvas, and measures 51 x 64in. Rousseau painted it in 1891 and showed it at an exhibition in Paris later that year.

About Rousseau

Henri Rousseau was born in France in 1844. He worked as a customs officer and painted in his spare time. The French for customs officer is *douanier*, so he was nicknamed Douanier Rousseau. At first, art critics laughed at his simple, self-taught style. But many artists admired it.

The Scream

This picture of a skeletal man clutching his head has become a famous image of pain and suffering. It was created by Norwegian artist Edvard Munch in 1893.

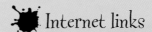 Internet links

For links to websites where you can see more pictures by Munch, go to www.usborne-quicklinks.com

Whose scream?

The man in the picture has his mouth open, so you might think it is him screaming. But Munch said the work was inspired by a scream that he felt, mysteriously, coming from the world around him.

One evening, Munch said, he went for a walk. As the sun set: "suddenly the sky turned blood red... I stood there shaking with fear and felt an endless scream passing through nature." The echoes of this terrifying noise are suggested by the strange, swirling lines in the picture.

About Munch

Edvard Munch was born in Norway in 1863. He had a sad childhood – his mother and eldest sister died tragically young, and he himself was often ill. He also lost his father and brother in the years that followed. So it comes as no surprise that many of his paintings are about sickness and death. Munch said he wanted to paint "living beings who breathe and feel and love and suffer" – as he must have done. His style of art was so expressive, it came to be known as Expressionism.

The face in the picture is so thin and shrunken, it's like a skull. Some people think it was based on a South American mummy Munch saw in a museum.

Munch created several versions of *The Scream*, some in color and some in black and white. This one dates from 1893. Munch made it using tempera paints and pastels on card stock. It measures 36 x 29in.

Edvard Munch 1893

The Kiss

This picture was painted between 1907 and 1908, by Austrian artist Gustav Klimt. He used oil paints and real gold leaf on a square canvas. The canvas measures 71 x 71in.

About Klimt

Gustav Klimt was born in Austria in 1862, the son of a gold and silver engraver. After studying art, he and his brother set up a successful business painting murals. But Gustav's pictures often shocked people, because of the sensuous way he drew women. In the end, he resigned from his official art jobs so he could pursue his own ideas more freely. He died in 1918.

Gold and jewels

The painting on the left is Klimt's most popular work – a dazzling, golden image of a man kissing a woman. But, apart from the carpet of jewel-like flowers, the background is strangely empty. This lack of setting makes the picture feel timeless. Only the couple's faces, hands and feet are clearly shown – the rest is lost in a swirl of patterned gold. The different patterns overlap and mingle, symbolizing the couple's closeness.

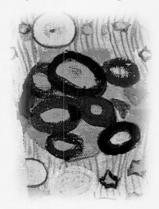

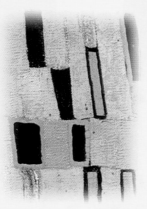

The woman's clothes have a flowery pattern, while the man's clothes are covered with rectangles.

A new art

Klimt's rich, decorative style is often linked to a movement known as Art Nouveau, which means "new art" in French. Art Nouveau was all about ornamental touches, especially flowery swirls and curls – not just in paintings, but in all kinds of art and design, including buildings, furniture and advertisements.

This poster is a good example of Art Nouveau. Dating from 1897, it was designed to advertise a magazine.

The Large Blue Horses

German artist Franz Marc loved animals and painted many different kinds – dogs, cats, cows, sheep, tigers and, especially, horses. For him, animals stood for a purer, more innocent way of life.

Animal magic

This picture shows a landscape with three horses painted in bold, unrealistic colors and simple, rounded shapes. The picture is as much about pattern and color as it is about how horses actually look. Marc wanted to express what he felt about the horses – their strength and spirit – rather than create a real-life scene.

About Marc

Franz Marc was born in Germany in 1880. He became known for his paintings of animals, and even gave lessons in animal anatomy. With his friend Kandinsky, he published a magazine named *The Blue Rider*. Marc was killed fighting in the First World War in 1914.

Marc painted *The Large Blue Horses* in 1911. He used oil paints on a large canvas measuring 42 x 71in. This is one of a series of horse pictures he painted at about this time.

The blue horses contrast vividly with the reds and yellows around them. But notice how the curved shapes of their bodies are echoed by the curves in the landscape, making them seem to fit in with their surroundings.

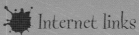 Internet links

For links to websites where you can see more pictures by Marc or color in your own horses, go to **www.usborne-quicklinks.com**

Improvisation No. 26 (Rowing)

At first glance, the painting on the right doesn't seem to be a picture of anything in particular. It just looks like a splotchy, abstract pattern made up by the artist. But in fact, it was loosely based on a view of two people in a boat – as the second part of its title, *Rowing*, hints.

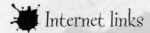 **Internet links**

For links to websites where you can explore more paintings by Kandinsky or create your own abstract art, go to
www.usborne-quicklinks.com

About Kandinsky

Vassily Kandinsky was born in Russia in 1866. He learned to play the piano and cello before studying law. It wasn't until his thirties that he went to Germany to study art. There, he met Franz Marc and became one of the earliest pioneers of what is known as "abstract" art – meaning art that does not mirror real people or things.

Kandinsky said he was inspired to experiment by seeing a painting that had fallen on its side – he thought the shapes in it looked more interesting seen sideways.

Improvised art?

Was this painting really made up on the spot, as the name *Improvisation* suggests? The answer is probably not. The artist, Vassily Kandinsky, usually did several sketches before creating a final painting. So all the shapes and colors were very carefully planned.

Music and color

Color was very important to Kandinsky. He thought color could express feelings in the same way as music. According to him, "Color is a power that directly influences the soul... Color is the keyboard... The artist is the hand that plays." Kandinsky even claimed that looking at colors made him hear musical sounds.

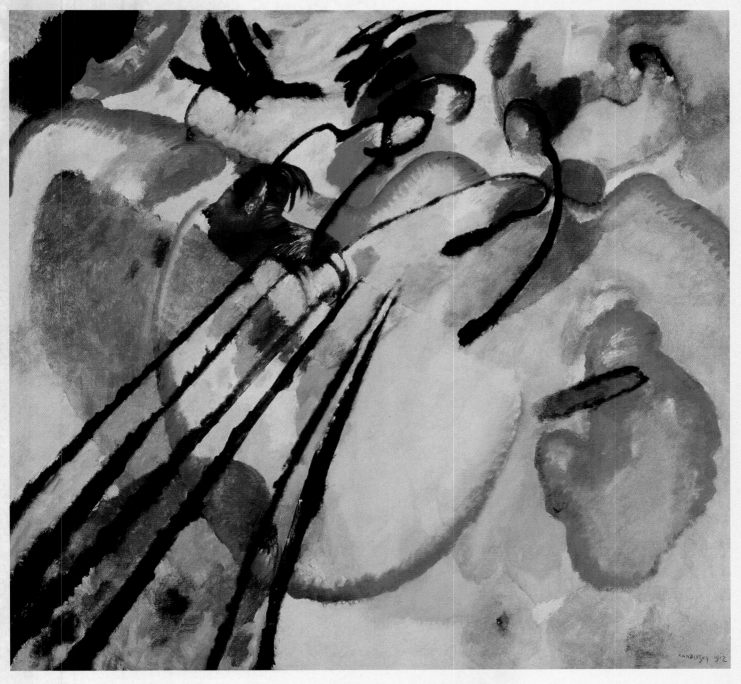

Vassily Kandinsky created *Improvisation No. 26 (Rowing)* in 1912. He used oil paints on a canvas measuring 38 x 43in.

Hidden clues

If you look closely, the picture contains several clues about the scene that inspired it. Can you make out a red curved line that might be a boat? Black lines hint at two people sitting in it, rowing with long, dark oars. The boat floats among dramatic splashes of color, suggesting a wild, watery setting. Above, a dark, bird-like shape flies through an equally colorful sky.

43

Three Musicians

Pablo Picasso painted *Three Musicians* in 1921, using oil paints on canvas. It measures 79 x 88in.

This colorful picture shows three musicians in old theatrical costumes. On the left, there is a clarinet player wearing a white pierrot suit (a pierrot was a kind of clown), with a dog behind him. In the middle is a guitarist dressed as a harlequin (another kind of clown). A singer in a monk's robe stands on the right.

Confusing cubes

In many ways, this is a confusing picture. The shapes overlap, so it is hard to tell where one thing stops and another starts. The space looks odd, too. The floor goes back further on the left than on the right, so the room seems strangely lopsided.

Picasso wasn't trying to create a lifelike picture. He wanted to draw attention to the problems involved in turning a real, 3-D scene into a flat, 2-D painting. So he distorted space and broke things up into angular shapes. This style, developed by Picasso and his friend Georges Braque, became known as Cubism.

About Picasso

Pablo Picasso was born in Spain in 1881. He became one of the most famous modern artists, working in many different styles – from delicate pastels to striking Cubist scenes. He even designed stage sets.

Picasso was a child prodigy. His mother said he could draw before he learned to talk.

Portrait of the artist

Picasso probably meant the masked harlequin to be a self portrait. Compared to this photograph of Picasso, it's hard to spot the likeness. But Picasso thought an artist was a kind of performer, like a harlequin, so he often used harlequins as a personal symbol.

Picasso loved jokes. This photograph, taken by Robert Doisneau in 1952, shows him pretending to have enormous, bread-roll fingers.

The House by the Railroad

American artist Edward Hopper painted this atmospheric view of a deserted house in 1925. He used oil paints on a canvas measuring 24 x 29in.

About Hopper

Edward Hopper was born in 1882. A shopkeeper's son, he grew up in a small American town, but moved to New York to become a painter. At first, he had to work as an illustrator to make ends meet. But later his paintings became very popular. People began to admire their moody atmosphere and distinctive American style. Hopper died in 1967.

Spooky scene

The house in Edward Hopper's painting looks spookily empty and remote. The windows are dark or hidden by blinds, and the entrance is lost in shadow. The railroad cuts across the scene, hiding any path to the door.

Hopper loved movies and his pictures often resemble movie scenes. In fact, *The House by the Railroad* probably inspired the creepy motel in Alfred Hitchcock's movie, *Psycho*. And it may also have inspired cartoonist Charles Addams, who invented the spooky "Addams Family."

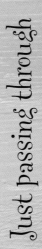

Charles Addams drew this cartoon in 1946. It shows the Addams Family pouring hot oil over some unsuspecting carol singers.

Just passing through

Hopper deliberately chose to paint a quirky, old-fashioned building – somewhere left behind by the times. It looks very realistic, but Hopper actually changed a lot of it. He left out part of the house and most of its surroundings. But he kept the railroad that hints at people just passing through. According to Hopper, "the most important thing is the sense of going on. You know how beautiful things are when you're traveling."

Abstraction White Rose

American artist Georgia O'Keeffe became famous for painting huge close-ups of flowers – lilies, roses, poppies and even weeds. Sometimes, she made the flowers so big that it is hard to recognize them.

Flower power

Talking about her flower paintings, O'Keeffe said, "Nobody sees a flower, really, it is so small. We haven't time – and to see takes time... So I said to myself: I'll paint what I see – what the flower is to me – but I'll paint it big... I'll make even busy New Yorkers take time to see what I see of flowers."

About O'Keeffe

Georgia O'Keeffe grew up on an American farm, determined to be an artist. In 1916, a friend showed some of her drawings to Alfred Steiglitz, who owned a gallery in New York. Impressed, he began to exhibit her work, and she quickly became a success. Later, O'Keeffe spent a lot of time in New Mexico, creating stark, beautiful images of the desert landscape and the sun-bleached bones she found there.

Internet links

For links to websites where you can see more paintings by O'Keeffe, or watch a flower opening in close-up, go to www.usborne-quicklinks.com

Almost abstract

The painting on the right shows a white rose as few people have ever seen one. The flower has been blown up to about 15 times life size, revealing the precise shape and subtle coloring of each petal.

The rose is seen from so close up that it fills the whole canvas, hiding any background. This lack of setting makes the picture seem almost abstract – as its title suggests. In fact, O'Keeffe helped to launch abstract art in America.

O'Keeffe painted *Abstraction White Rose* in 1927, using oil paints on a canvas measuring 36 x 30in.

Splatter paintings

One of the best-known modern artists is Jackson Pollock. He became famous for making huge abstract pictures by dripping, splattering and splashing paint – a technique that earned him the nickname Jack the Dripper.

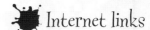 Internet links

For links to websites where you can see more Pollock pictures and watch a movie of him at work, go to www.usborne-quicklinks.com

Action man

Pollock applied paint in a variety of ways. He dipped brushes in paint and flicked them. He pierced paint cans and swung them over his canvas. And he squeezed oil paints straight from the tube to create thick, ridged lines. Sometimes, he added sand, glass or cigarette butts for texture. Because his method was so physical, art critics began to call it Action Painting.

About Pollock

Jackson Pollock was born in the U.S. in 1912. He went to New York to study art, and became a prominent member of the art scene there.

Like many artists at the time, Pollock believed art should be a way of expressing feelings. Together, these artists are known as Abstract Expressionists. Pollock was killed in a car crash at the age of 44.

This photograph shows how Pollock liked to paint, using a huge canvas laid flat on the floor.

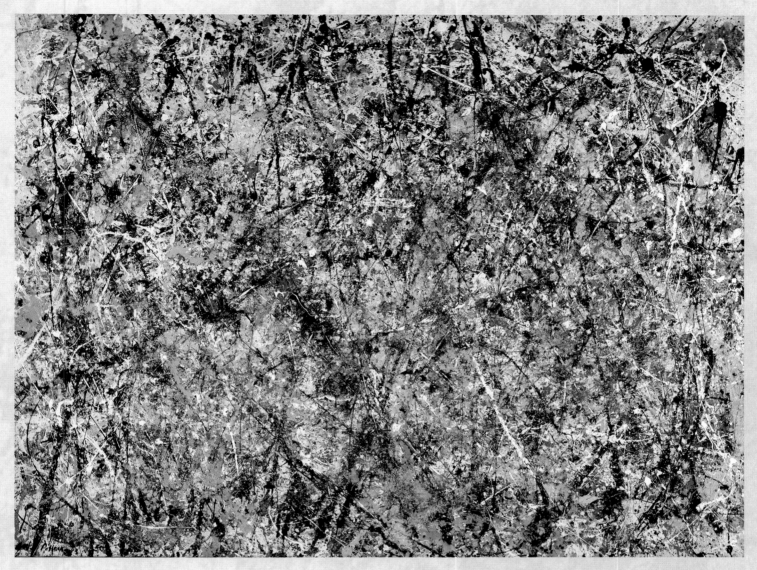

Pollock painted *Lavender Mist* in 1950. It measures an enormous 87 x 118in.

Lavender Mist

Pollock originally called this picture *Number 1, 1950*. He often gave his pictures numbers rather than names, because they weren't pictures of other things. But his friend, the art critic Clement Greenberg, suggested he call it *Lavender Mist*, because of its hazy effect and the way the touches of gray, blue and pink suggest the color of lavender flowers. The colors are overlaid with tangled streaks of black and white. The dense pattern gives you a feeling of restless energy and spontaneous rhythm. It might look messy, but Pollock said he was in control of every splatter, splash and dribble. In his pictures, he insisted, "There is no accident."

51

The Snail

 French artist Henri Matisse made *The Snail* in 1953. It measures a huge 113 x 113in – that's taller than a person. The picture is made up of cutout paper shapes. Matisse's assistant colored the paper by painting it with bright gouache paints.

Hidden clue

At first glance, this picture looks like just a pattern of colored blocks. But there is more to it than that – as the title *Snail* suggests. Matisse arranged the blocks in a spiral shape, like that of a spiral snail shell. And there is another clue hidden in the picture. If you look closely at the lilac shape in the top left hand corner, you will see a tiny snail shape jutting out of the top.

A spiral snail shell, of the kind that inspired Matisse

Matisse thought art should be pleasant and relaxing, "like a good armchair."

About Matisse

Henri Matisse was born in 1869 in France. He was going to be a lawyer, but then became ill. While he was recovering, his mother bought him a box of paints to entertain him – and he was hooked. He gave up law and became an artist. To start with, his bold use of color shocked some people – but he is now admired as one of the greatest artists of his time.

Drawing with scissors

By the time he made this picture, Matisse was over 80 and too ill to paint. So he came up with a new technique using colored paper. Matisse cut shapes out of the paper – he called this "drawing with scissors." With his assistant's help, the shapes were then arranged and glued down. This method is known as collage, from *colle*, the French word for "glue."

This photo shows Matisse in bed, cutting out shapes for one of his collage pictures.

Surreal scenes

Belgian painter René Magritte specialized in paintings of strange, imaginary scenes, often involving men in bowler hats. This one has hundreds of them hovering in the air above an ordinary-looking street.

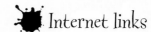 Internet links

For links to websites where you can view more weird works by Magritte and other Surrealists, go to **www.usborne-quicklinks.com**

Magritte painted this scene, *Golconda*, in 1953. He used oil paints on a canvas of 32 x 40in. "Golconda" was the name of a fabulously rich ancient city, but came to mean anything that makes a lot of money. So perhaps Magritte meant the title to refer to a more modern source of wealth – city workers.

Tales of the unexpected

The men float impossibly in the sky, or perhaps rain out of it – but they seem to find this completely natural. They stand casually in thin air, dressed in suits and hats, like old-fashioned city workers on their way to the office.

Despite the strangeness of the scene, Magritte painted it in a very lifelike way. It is only the combination of things that makes it look absurd. Magritte loved painting ordinary things in extraordinary situations. He said he wanted to play with the viewer's expectations in order to "challenge the real world."

More than real

Magritte's pictures formed an important part of an art movement known as Surrealism. Surrealist works were not meant to be un-real but *more* than real, or "*sur*-real" (*sur* is French for "above").

The Surrealists wanted to create strange images in order to startle viewers into new ways of thinking about the world. They saw beauty in the most bizarre, unexpected combinations of things, such as a lobster and a telephone.

Famous Spanish Surrealist Salvador Dalí created *Lobster Telephone* in 1936, using a plaster lobster and a real phone.

About Magritte

René Magritte was born in Belgium in 1898. After studying art, he earned a living designing ads and wallpaper. But he was also painting. After meeting other Surrealists, he began creating the bizarre images for which he is now famous.

Magritte was a shy man who often wore a bowler hat himself.

Campbell's Soup Can (Tomato)

Andy Warhol is famous for his bright, stylish prints of everything from cola bottles to movie stars. One of his favorite subjects was canned soup. He made hundreds and hundreds of prints of cans, in various colors and flavors.

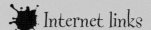 Internet links

For links to websites where you can find out more about printmaking and Warhol, go to www.usborne-quicklinks.com

About Warhol

Andy Warhol was born in the United States in 1928. He began his career as a commercial artist and many of his most famous pictures draw on his knowledge of advertising and design.

Warhol was fascinated by famous faces and carefully created a celebrity image of his own, wearing a wild white wig to make sure he stood out from other people. In 1968, he was shot and nearly killed by a former assistant. He died in 1987.

Warhol also made experimental films, including a six-hour film of a man sleeping and an eight-hour film of the Empire State Building.

Factory-made art

By specializing in printing, Warhol could make multiple copies of his pictures. He didn't hold with the old idea that each work of art should be one of a kind, individually crafted by the artist. He even named his studio "The Factory," to encourage people to compare his art to manufacturing.

Pop rebel

Warhol's pictures are often described as Pop art. Pop was an art movement inspired by the popular culture of the 1950s and 60s, with its glossy magazines, pop music, television, films and advertisements. Pop artists copied from these sources to create bright, appealing images – which were at the same time a wry comment on modern values.

Campbell's Soup Can (Tomato) by Andy Warhol. Warhol created this print in 1965. It measures 36 x 24in.

Warhol's colorful prints became so well known that the Campbell Soup Company produced a special series of soup cans to commemorate him.

Pearblossom Highway

This shimmering view of a Californian highway was created by British artist David Hockney. It is full of photographic detail – but it is far from an ordinary photograph. In fact, it is hundreds of photos stuck together.

Multiple views

Each photo in *Pearblossom Highway* shows just a tiny piece of the whole scene. Because the photos don't match exactly, everything seems oddly broken up. The sky is patchy, parts of the road signs are repeated, and the edges of the road wobble around. Hockney plays with the variations in color and shape, revealing how photos can be chosen to shape and distort what they show.

About Hockney

David Hockney was born in England in 1937, but he moved to California in the 1960s and has worked there ever since. He was first known as a painter, but has also experimented with making art out of anything from photos to fax-machine printouts.

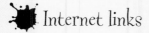 Internet links

For a link to a website where you can take a tour of
Hockney's pictures, go to **www.usborne-quicklinks.com**

David Hockney made this collage in April 1986,
using hundreds of snapshots taken in California.
The collage measures 78 x 111in.

Glossary

People use a lot of specialized words to talk about art. This glossary explains some of the words you will find in this book – or that you may come across elsewhere.

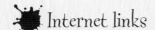 **Internet links**
For links to art websites with more useful explanations and quizzes, go to www.usborne-quicklinks.com

2-D or **two-dimensional** – things that look flat. For example, a square is a 2-D shape.

3-D or **three-dimensional** – things that look (or are) solid. For example, a cube is a 3-D shape.

abstract art – art that does not mirror real people or things, but is an arrangement of shapes and colors.

Abstract Expressionists – a group of New York artists of the 1940s-50s, including Jackson Pollock. They made abstract works meant to express their feelings.

Action painting – a way of painting by splashing and dripping paint with energetic movements. It was made famous by Jackson Pollock.

art – things made to be looked at, especially paintings and sculptures. It can also be used to describe anything creative, including music and poetry.

art movement – a group of artists who work together and share ideas, and often hold joint exhibitions.

Art Nouveau – an art and design movement of the 1890s, known for flowery, decorative patterns, as in the work of Gustav Klimt.

canvas – rough cloth used for painting on, usually stretched over a wooden frame.

collages – pictures made by gluing down pieces of paper, cloth or other materials.

color wheel – an arrangement of colors that shows how to mix the primary colors to create new colors. You can see a picture of it on page 33.

complementary colors – colors that lie opposite each other on the color wheel. Seen side by side, they contrast very strongly and make each other look brighter.

cool colors – colors that give a sense of cold, such as blue and white.

Cubism – a style that draws attention to the problems involved in making a flat, 2-D image of a real, 3-D scene. It was developed in Paris around 1907, by Pablo Picasso and his friend Georges Braque.

Expressionism – an early 20th-century style developed in Germany. Expressionist artists use exaggerated shapes and colors to try to convey feelings, as in the work of Edvard Munch.

frescos – wall paintings made by painting onto wet plaster.

gouache – thick, water-based paints.

Impressionism – an art movement founded in France in the 1870s, by Claude Monet and his friends. They painted outdoors and developed a sketchy, "impressionistic" style, to try to capture the changing effects of natural light.

murals – wall paintings.

oil paintings – paintings made using oil paints.

oil paints or **oils** – slow-drying, oil-based paints.

palette – a board on which an artist mixes paint colors.

pastel drawings – drawings made using pastels.

pastels – soft, colored crayons.

Pointillism – a painting technique developed around 1855 by Georges Seurat, using tiny dots of pure, unmixed colors. Seen from a distance the dots seem to merge, creating the effect of blended colors.

Pop art – a mid-20th-century British and American art movement that used images from pop culture, such as comic strips and adverts. Andy Warhol was a famous Pop artist.

Pre-Raphaelite Brotherhood – a group of British artists, founded in 1848, who wanted to make art that was truer to nature and more spiritual. They included John Millais.

Primary colors – red, yellow and blue. All other colors can be made by mixing these colors together in different amounts.

prints – pictures made using a carved block or a stencil (a template with holes cut in it). With a block, the carved area is coated with ink and pressed against paper. With a stencil, the stencil is laid over paper and spread with ink, so the ink prints through the holes. Both methods allow artists to make lots of copies of a picture.

Renaissance – a period in the 15th and 16th centuries when there were lots of new discoveries in art and science.

Romantics – a group of late 18th and early 19th-century artists, including Caspar David Friedrich, who were inspired by a love of nature.

sculpture – a statue or 3-D work of art.

secondary colors – orange, green and purple, the colors you get when you mix two primary colors together.

still life – a picture of flowers or food, or other unmoving objects. The plural is "still lifes" (not "lives").

Surrealism – a 20th-century art movement which used bizarre, dream-like images. René Magritte and Salvador Dalí were famous Surrealists.

tempera – fast-drying, egg-based paints.

warm colors – colors that give a sense of warmth, such as red and orange.

watercolors – transparent, water-based paints. They come in tubes or in solid blocks known as "pans."

Using the Internet

What you do

To visit a recommended site:

- 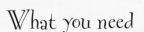 Go to **www.usborne-quicklinks.com**
- Type the keywords **"childrens art"**
- Select the page number
- Click on the link

What you need

All the websites described in this book can be accessed with a standard home computer and a web browser (the software that lets you look at information from the Internet). Some sites need extra programs (plug-ins) to play sound or show videos or animations. You can download these plug-ins for free from the Internet.

If you go to a site and do not have the necessary plug-in, a message will come up on the screen. There is usually a button on the site that you can click on to download the plug-in. Alternatively, go to Usborne Quicklinks and click on "Net Help". There, you will find links to download plug-ins.

Note for parents

The websites described in this book are regularly reviewed and the links in Usborne Quicklinks are updated. However, the content of a website may change at any time and Usborne Publishing is not responsible for the content of any website other than its own. We recommend that children are supervised while on the Internet, that they do not use Internet chat rooms, and that parents and guardians use Internet filtering software to block unsuitable material. Please ensure that children read and follow the safety guidelines printed above. For more information, see the "Net Help" area on the Usborne Quicklinks Website.

Internet safety

When using the Internet, please make sure you follow these guidelines:

- Ask permission from your parent or guardian before connecting to the Internet.

- When you are on the Internet, never tell anyone your full name, address or telephone number. Ask an adult before giving your email address.

- If a website asks you to log in or register by typing your name or email address, ask an adult's permission first.

- If you do receive an email from someone you don't know, do not reply to the email – just delete it.

Site availability

The links in Usborne Quicklinks are regularly reviewed and updated, but occasionally you may get a message that a site is unavailable. This might be temporary, so try again later, or even the next day.

Websites do occasionally close down and, when this happens, we will replace them with new links in Usborne Quicklinks. Sometimes we add extra links too, if we think they are interesting. So when you visit Usborne Quicklinks, the links may be slightly different from those described in your book.

Acknowledgements

Sample paintwork and textures by Antonia Miller and Katie Lovell.
Picture research by Ruth King. Digital manipulation by Nick Wakeford and John Russell.
Cover design by Mary Cartwright. Additional design work by Louise Flutter.
Edited by Jane Chisholm and Jenny Tyler. Additional Internet research by Alex Frith.

Every effort has been made to trace the copyright holders of the material in this book. If any rights have been omitted, the publishers offer their sincere apologies and will rectify this in any subsequent editions following notification. The publishers are grateful to the following organisations and individuals for their contributions and permission to reproduce material:

Cover: (top left) detail of paintwork by Katie Lovell; (bottom left) detail from *Tiger in a Tropical Storm*, see credit for pages 34-35; (middle) *The Water Lily Pond*, see credit for pages 28-29; (top right) detail from *Sunflowers*, see credit for pages 30-31; (bottom right) detail from *The Birth of Venus*, see credit for pages 10-11. **Title page:** detail from *The Circus*, see credit for pages 32-33. **Contents page:** detail from *The Milkmaid*, see credit for pages 14-15. Pages 4-5: *Tobias and the Angel* by the workshop of Verocchio (National Gallery, London) © National Gallery Collection; By kind permission of the Trustees of the National Gallery, London/ CORBIS. Detail from *The Birth of Venus*, see credit for pages 10-11. Detail from *The Large Blue Horses*, see credit for pages 40-41. **Pages 6-7:** Photograph of artist's palette © James Marshall/ CORBIS. *Man in a Turban* by Jan van Eyck (National Gallery, London) © National Gallery Collection; By kind permission of the Trustees of the National Gallery, London/ CORBIS. **Pages 8-9:** *Mona Lisa* by Leonardo (Musée du Louvre, Paris) © Gianni Dagli Orti/ CORBIS. Detail of the Sistine Chapel ceiling by Michelangelo (Vatican Palace, Rome) © Bettmann/ CORBIS. **Pages 10-11:** *The Birth of Venus* by Botticelli (Uffizi Gallery, Florence) main image and rose detail © Summerfield Press/ CORBIS. Venus detail © Francis G. Mayer/ CORBIS. **Pages 12-13:** *Hunters in the Snow* by Bruegel (Kunsthistorisches Museum, Vienna) © Kunsthistorisches Museum, Vienna/ Bridgeman Art Library. **Pages 14-15:** *The Artist in his Studio* by Rembrandt (Museum of Fine Arts, Boston) Zoe Oliver Sherman Collection given in memory of Lillie Oliver Poor, 38.1838 © 2005 Museum of Fine Arts, Boston; All rights reserved/ Bridgeman Art Library. *The Milkmaid* by Vermeer (Rijksmuseum, Amsterdam) © Rijksmuseum, Amsterdam/ Bridgeman Art Library. **Pages 16-17:** *Fruit and Flowers in a Teracotta Vase* by van Os (National Gallery, London) © National Gallery Collection; By kind permission of the Trustees of the National Gallery, London/ CORBIS. **Pages 18-19:** *Doña Isabel de Porcel* by Goya (National Gallery, London) © National Gallery Collection; By kind permission of the Trustees of the National Gallery, London/ CORBIS. *Neither More Nor Less* by Goya (from *Los Caprichos*, no. 41) © Burstein Collection/ CORBIS. **Pages 20-21:** *Wanderer Above the Sea of Fog* (Kunsthalle, Hamburg) © Archivo Iconografico, S.A./ CORBIS. **Pages 22-23:** *Ophelia* by John Millais (Tate Gallery, London) © The Art Archive/ Tate Gallery London/ Eileen Tweedy. **Pages 24-25:** *Nocturne in Blue and Silver: Battersea Reach* by James Whistler (Isabella Stewart Gardner Museum, Boston) © Burstein Collection/ CORBIS. The *"Fighting Temeraire" Tugged to Her Last Berth to be Broken Up, 1838* by Turner (National Gallery, London) © National Gallery Collection; By kind permission of the Trustees of the National Gallery, London/ CORBIS. **Pages 26-27:** *Little Dancer Aged Fourteen* by Degas (Philadelphia Museum of Art) © Philadelphia Museum of Art/ CORBIS. *Dancer on the Stage* by Degas (Musée d'Orsay, Paris); © Archivo Iconografico, S.A./ CORBIS. **Pages 28-29:** *The Water Lily Pond* by Monet (National Gallery, London) © National Gallery Collection; By kind permission of the Trustees of the National Gallery, London/ CORBIS. Photograph of Monet's garden at Giverny, France by Sund © Getty Images. **Pages 30-31:** *Sunflowers* by van Gogh (Neue Pinakothek, Munich) © Neue Pinakothek, Munich/ Bridgeman Art Library. *Van Gogh painting Sunflowers* by Gauguin (Van Gogh Museum, Amsterdam) © Archivo Iconografico, S.A./ CORBIS. **Pages 32-33:** *The Circus* by Seurat (Musée d'Orsay, Paris) © Edimédia/ CORBIS. Detail of clown © Francis G. Mayer/ CORBIS. **Pages 34-35:** *Tiger in a Tropical Storm – Surprise!* by Rousseau (National Gallery, London) © National Gallery Collection; By kind permission of the Trustees of the National Gallery, London/ CORBIS. **Pages 36-37:** *The Scream* by Munch (Munch Museum, Oslo) © J. Lathion/ National Gallery Norway/ Munch Museum/ Munch-Ellingsen Group, BONO, Oslo/ DACS, London 2005. **Pages 38-39:** *The Kiss* by Klimt (Österreichische Galerie, Vienna) © Austrian Archives; Österreichische Galerie, Vienna/ CORBIS. Art nouveau poster by Berthon © Archivo Iconografico, S.A./ CORBIS. **Pages 40-41:** *The Large Blue Horses* by Marc (Walker Art Center, Minneapolis) © Collection Walker Art Center, Minneapolis, Gift of the T. B. Walker Foundation, Gilbert M. Walker Fund, 1942. **Pages 42-43:** *Improvisation No. 26 (Rowing)* by Kandinsky (Stadtische Galerie im Lenbachhaus, Munich) © Stadtische Galerie im Lenbachhaus, Munich/ Bridgeman Art Library/ ADAGP, Paris and DACS, London 2005. **Pages 44-45:** *Three Musicians* by Picasso (Museum of Modern Art, New York) © Lauros/ Giraudon/ Bridgeman Art Library/ Succession Picasso/ DACS 2005. Photograph of Picasso by Doisneau © Robert Doisneau/ Rapho/ Network Photographers. **Pages 46-47:** *The House by the Railroad* by Hopper (Museum of Modern Art, New York) © Museum of Modern Art, New York/ Bridgeman Art Library. Addams Family cartoon by Charles Addams © Tee and Charles Addams Foundation. **Pages 48-49:** *Abstraction White Rose* by O'Keeffe (Georgia O'Keeffe Museum, Santa Fe) © Photo SCALA, Florence/ Georgia O'Keeffe Museum, Santa Fe/ DACS, London 2005. **Pages 50-51:** *Lavender Mist: Number 1, 1950* by Pollock (National Gallery of Art, Washington DC) © National Gallery of Art, Washington DC/ Bridgeman Art Library/ ARS, NY and DACS, London 2005. Photograph of Pollock © Rex Features. **Pages 52-53:** *The Snail* by Matisse (Tate Gallery, London) © The Art Archive/ Tate Gallery London/ Eileen Tweedy © Succession H. Matisse/ DACS 2005. Photograph of snail shell © Digital Vision. Photograph of Matisse © Bettmann/ CORBIS. **Pages 54-55:** *Golconda* by Magritte (Menil Collection, Houston) © Lauros/ Giraudon/ Bridgeman Art Library/ ADAGP, Paris and DACS, London 2005. Photograph of Magritte by Duane Michals, New York ca. 1965, Tirage Dulière, non vintage, MRBAB, AACB, inv. 9881; By kind permission of the Fine Arts Museum, Belgium. **Pages 56-57:** *Campbell's Soup Can (Tomato)* by Andy Warhol (Andy Warhol Foundation, New York) Image © Andy Warhol Foundation/ CORBIS, Artwork © The Andy Warhol Foundation for the Visual Arts/ Corbis. **Pages 58-59:** *Pearblossom Highway, 11th-18th April 1986 (Second Version)* by Hockney (J. Paul Getty Museum, Los Angeles) © David Hockney.

Index